Very SALAD DRESSING

Very SALAD DRESSING

TERESA BURNS

CELESTIAL ARTS
Berkeley

Copyright © 1997, 2004 by Teresa Burns
Cover photographs copyright © 2004 by Maren Caruso

Library of Congress Cataloging-in-Publication Data
Burns, Teresa H.
  Very salad dressing / Teresa Burns. — [Rev. ed.].
    p. cm.
  Rev. ed. of: Salad dressings. Freedom, CA : Crossing Press, c1987.
  1. Salad dressing. I. Burns, Teresa H. Salad dressings. II. Title.
  TX819.S27B89 2004
    641.8'14—dc22
2004006117

ISBN-13: 978-1-58761-209-1 (pbk.)

Printed in Malaysia

Cover design by Nancy Austin and Chloe Rawlins based
on an original design by Susanne Weihl
Text design by Chloe Rawlins based on an original design
by Susanne Weihl

15 14 13

First Revised Edition

Contents

Introduction

Salad is my passion. For the last several years, salad and the consumption of vegetables have been an American fascination as well. There's no reason not to make your own salad dressings. I hope that these recipes inspire you to be creative and to have fun with everyday cooking: there are no complicated cooking steps to follow. Just look at the recipes and the list of ingredients—they are short and simple. This chapter will give you a few tips for making salad dressings to make the process even easier and more convenient.

EQUIPMENT

I have a hand blender—also called an immersion blender— that I use for making most dressings. This small hand-held appliance is a portable blender with enough power to chop ingredients, such as garlic or onion, while blending the liquids. Hand blenders often come with different attachments for blending, whipping, and chopping, but the blending attachment alone works for all salad-dressing chores. Also, they often come with their own clear plastic and/or stainless steel mixing containers. These are especially convenient since you can serve directly from the containers, further reducing cleanup time. If your hand blender doesn't have its own container, you can substitute any wide-mouth jar or measuring cup and get the same quick and easy results.

Of course, you can use a food processor for making most dressings, but food processors do present some disadvantages. First, a blender will incorporate more air into a dressing than a food processor; therefore, food-processor dressings are a little heavier and have less volume. The other disadvantage is that you will have to transfer the dressing to another container— more dishes to wash.

Most vinaigrettes can be made with a bowl, a whisk, and a little wrist action. Or use a portable hand mixer with just one mixer blade in place in a tall, wide-mouth jar and you have something that works almost as well as a hand blender. The mixing blades don't do a good job of chopping, so you will have to chop the herbs, garlic, onion, and other such ingredients on a cutting board and add to the dressing before or after mixing.

You also need a grater for grating Parmesan cheese, a pepper mill for freshly ground pepper, and a reamer for juicing small quantities of citrus fruits.

INGREDIENTS

Your cupboard should contain an assortment of oils, vinegars, and dried herbs.

Oils You may think there's a lot of oil in some of these dressings. That's true, but you only need about 1 tablespoon of dressing per serving, and that turns out to be a very moderate amount of fat.

I like the idea of being able to pick the oil for a recipe. Any oil works. You might choose an extra virgin olive oil when you want a rich taste. I like the rich, fruity, almost peppery flavor it gives to a dressing. Nut oils are delicately flavored and balance the bitter flavor of some greens. Nut oils turn rancid quickly, so it is a good idea to buy them in small bottles and store them in the refrigerator. Peanut oil, sesame oil, and safflower oil are also good. Toasted sesame oil, made from toasted seeds, is dark in color and great with dressings that contain soy sauce. Sesame oil, made from raw sesame seeds, is light in both color and flavor. When a recipe calls for the unspecific "any vegetable oil," you may use any number of neutral-tasting oils or oil blends. Canola and grapeseed oil are good choices because they are monounsaturated oils and have a nice, light taste.

Vinegars and Citrus Juices Vinegar or lemon juice or both are used in most dressings to balance the oil. Red and white wine vinegar are made from grapes that were first made into wine. Cider vinegar comes from apples and rice vinegar comes from rice. I love the mildly sweet, apple flavor of cider vinegar and use it frequently. It is less expensive than the trendy balsamic vinegar and adds a wonderful flavor to a dressing. It's particularly good in coleslaw.

Rice vinegar is less acidic than other vinegars. Japanese rice vinegars tend to be sweet, while Chinese rice vinegars are more acidic.

Balsamic vinegar is an Italian red wine vinegar made by boiling the juice of Trebbiano grapes until the sugars caramelize. Then it is aged in oak barrels, like fine wines. The result is a vinegar with a mellow, almost sweet flavor and very dark color. If you aren't paying a premium price for balsamic vinegar, you are getting a cheap imitation made of red wine vinegar flavored with sugar, vanilla, and caramel coloring. Red wine vinegar retains the aroma of the wine from which it is made and is a fairly assertive flavor. White wine vinegar is more delicate and almost neutral in color.

Citrus juices also can be used to add tartness to a dressing. I use freshly squeezed lemon juice to bring a fresh, sharp tart flavor to my dressings. Lime juice can also be used, but it is more fruity and less acidic. To get more juice from a lemon or a lime, microwave it for 15 seconds on high and then press and roll it on a countertop a few times before juicing. Orange juice and grapefruit juice also can be used to add a citrusy tartness to a dressing.

There are two types of vinegar I don't use in salad dressings. White vinegar gives a pure, sharp flavor that is fine in pickles but doesn't contribute any flavor to a dressing. I also avoid malt vinegar, which is made from beer, because it has a very strong flavor that doesn't blend well with most dressing ingredients.

Yogurt, buttermilk, vinegar, and lemon juice all will add to the tartness side of the equation. You can balance the tartness with additional oil, or you can use a sweetener.

Mayonnaise and Dairy Products Sometimes a creamy texture is called for, and that's when mayonnaise, sour cream, yogurt, buttermilk, and/or cheese are used. I use reduced-fat mayonnaise. Those with a sensitive palate will probably notice when their favorite sandwich is made with a reduced-fat mayonnaise, but it generally goes unnoticed in a salad dressing. Of course, you can use regular mayonnaise or fat-free mayonnaise if you prefer.

Sour cream is made from cream that has been cultured with lactic acid. It is rich and adds great body and flavor to a dressing.

You can substitute reduced-fat or fat-free sour cream or yogurt, but taste the dressing. You may have to reduce the quantity of lemon juice or vinegar.

Cottage cheese that has been blended until smooth can be substituted for either yogurt or sour cream. Be sure to taste the dressing and add more vinegar if needed.

Parmesan cheese adds both body and flavor to a dressing. Always use freshly grated Parmesan.

Herbs When fresh herbs are available, they are a better choice than dried herbs. Unless otherwise stated, I measure fresh herbs by loosely packing the leaves into a measuring cup or spoon. The tough stems are discarded. The chopping can be done with a hand blender after you have measured out the correct amount.

Of all the herbs I use, parsley shows up most frequently, adding a fresh, green flavor to dressings. Both the curly-leaf type and a flat-leaf (Italian) type are available in supermarkets. The latter has a much stronger flavor.

To store fresh herbs, wrap them loosely in a damp paper towel, seal in a plastic bag, and keep in the refrigerator for up to 5 days. A bunch of herbs will also keep well in a small vase of water placed out of direct sunlight.

Garlic is another flavor I enjoy in most dressings. If you use a hand blender, you don't even have to bother with mincing or pressing the garlic before combining with the other ingredients.

Anchovies and Worcestershire Sauce You can't have a proper Caesar salad without anchovies, right? Anchovies or anchovy paste add a briny, pungent flavor to salad dressings. Use either sparingly. Rather than chop the fish, or deal with the leftovers in the can, I prefer anchovy paste in convenient squeeze tubes.

Worcestershire sauce adds a dark, rich, briny, sweet flavor to dressings. It is not as pungent as anchovies, but acts in a similar way to balance the tart ingredients. Worcestershire sauce is made from garlic, soy sauce, tamarind, onions, molasses, lime, anchovies, vinegar, and various spices.

Salt and Pepper I rarely specify an exact quantity of salt and pepper. Your taste and your dietary requirements should guide you. I do recommend that you don't omit these important flavors altogether.

In my pepper grinder, I keep a mix of white, black, and red peppercorns. I use it on everything, including salad dressings. It adds quite a bit of flavor.

Eggs Several recipes call for eggs, both raw and hard-cooked. In both cases, the eggs are essential for flavor and texture. Raw eggs are added as an emulsifier in many oil-and-vinegar dressings. Vinegar is water-based and won't mix with oil unless you help it along. You can beat the two together to disperse the oil droplets in the vinegar. The second you stop beating, however, the oil and vinegar will separate. Mustard helps to emulsify the mixture, keeping the oil molecules suspended in the vinegar. But an egg yolk works even better. The drawback to raw eggs is the salmonella issue. Farmers and egg producers have been unable to eradicate the salmonella bacteria from their chickens, hence some raw eggs do present a health risk. To coddle an egg—reducing the risk of salmonella poisoning—place the egg, still in its shell, in boiling water for 60 seconds and remove immediately. Very often, the egg is an important part of a dressing (Sweet-and-Sour Salad Dressing on page 52, for example) and should not be omitted.

The danger of salmonella is greatest for the elderly, infants, pregnant women, and people with illnesses or compromised immune systems. Healthy adults should use discretion when it comes to eating raw eggs. Dressings made with raw eggs should be consumed on the day they are made.

Leftover egg whites can be stored for up to 4 days in a covered glass container in the refrigerator. They can be frozen for up to 1 year. Leftover egg yolks can be covered with water and stored in a covered glass jar for 2 to 3 days. Drain off the water before using.

Hard-cooked eggs present no such health risk. They add a rich flavor and creamy texture to several dressings. Dressings with hard-cooked eggs are particularly well suited to cooked vegetables such as asparagus or green beans.

TIPS

Cooks who make a lot of soups and stews know that their food often tastes better on the second day. The same holds true for salad dressings. Most of the recipes in this chapter make enough for two or more meals. You can enjoy them on the day they are made, then enjoy them even more on the second day, or you can make them in advance and serve them a day or two later.

Salad dressings should always be stored in an airtight container in the refrigerator. If your dressing has been chilling for more than an hour, it is best to take it out of the refrigerator about 5 minutes before you plan to serve it. Taste the dressing before you put it on the table. You may find that you need to add a little more oil or vinegar because you prefer a different balance between the two or because the flavor of the onion or garlic is threatening to overwhelm the dressing. The flavor of citrus juice sometimes fades and needs to be brightened by an addition of fresh juice. A little more salt often brings the flavors back into balance.

Minor changes in ingredients can make major differences in flavor. Feel free to experiment with different oils, different vinegars, or herbs.

USING SALAD DRESSINGS AS MARINADES

Many oil-and-vinegar dressings can do double duty as a marinade. In a marinade, the oils help food retain moisture by sealing the surface. The acid (wine, vinegar, or citrus juice) breaks down the tough fibers of the meat and helps to tenderize. The herbs and spices add flavor.

The rule of thumb is to marinate small cuts of meat for about 1 hour before cooking. Marinate large roasts and cuts of meat for several hours or overnight. Firm-fleshed fish and seafood should be marinated for about 30 minutes. Don't overdo the marinating time or you will turn your meat into mush!

Only reuse a marinade that has come in contact with raw meat after boiling it for 3 minutes over medium-high heat and, even then, only for basting meat, chicken, or fish during cooking. It must otherwise be discarded.

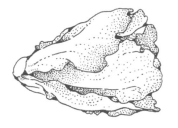

Oil-and-Vinegar Salad Dressings and Marinades

Mom's Dressing and Marinade

I learned how to make this very good, basic vinaigrette from my mother. Fines herbes, a mixture of very finely chopped dried herbs, flavors the dressing. The classic combination for the herb blend is chervil, chives, parsley, and tarragon.

$^1/_4$ cup red wine vinegar
1 tablespoon freshly squeezed lemon juice
2 cloves garlic, minced
2 teaspoons Dijon mustard
2 teaspoons sugar
1 teaspoon dried fines herbes
$^2/_3$ cup any vegetable oil
Salt and freshly ground pepper

In a small bowl, combine the vinegar, lemon juice, garlic, mustard, sugar, and herbs. Whisk to mix well. Slowly add the oil while whisking, and continue whisking until the mixture is emulsified. Or combine the ingredients in a jar and blend with a hand blender. Add salt and pepper to taste. Cover and chill the dressing until you are ready to use it. Let stand at room temperature for 5 minutes before whisking again and serving.

This dressing will keep for up to 4 days in an airtight container in the refrigerator.

Makes about 1 cup

Basic Herb Vinaigrette

Any herb will taste delicious in this basic vinaigrette—oregano, basil, thyme, savory, dill—whatever you have on hand. Fresh herbs pack more punch than dried, but dried herbs are okay, too. This versatile vinaigrette can dress any kind of salad—green and leafy, crunchy vegetable, even potato or chicken. It is also a fine marinade for beef, pork, lamb, poultry, or fish.

$^1/_4$ cup red wine vinegar
1 tablespoon chopped fresh oregano,
   or $^3/_4$ teaspoon dried
1 small clove garlic, minced
$^3/_4$ teaspoon dry mustard
$^1/_2$ teaspoon freshly squeezed lemon juice
$^1/_2$ teaspoon sugar
$^3/_4$ cup extra virgin olive oil
Salt and freshly ground pepper

In a small bowl, combine the vinegar, oregano, garlic, mustard, lemon juice, and sugar. Whisk to mix well. Slowly add the oil while whisking, and continue whisking until the mixture is emulsified. Add salt and pepper to taste. Cover and chill the dressing until you are ready to use it. Let stand at room temperature for 5 minutes before whisking again and serving.

You can save time by not chopping the oregano or mincing the garlic. Simply put everything in a 2-cup or 4-cup glass measuring cup and use a hand blender.

This dressing will keep for up to 4 days in an airtight container in the refrigerator.

Makes about 1 cup

Summertime Herb Vinaigrette

Like the previous recipe, this versatile recipe can dress any type of salad or be used as a marinade for any type of meat or fish.

2 $^1/_2$ tablespoons red wine vinegar
1 $^1/_2$ tablespoons Dijon mustard
1 tablespoon dry white wine
1 tablespoon chopped fresh thyme, or $^3/_4$ teaspoon dried
1 tablespoon chopped fresh oregano, or $^3/_4$ teaspoon dried
1 clove garlic, minced
$^1/_4$ cup any vegetable oil
Salt and freshly ground pepper

In a small bowl, combine the vinegar, mustard, wine, herbs, and garlic. Whisk to mix well. Slowly add the oil while whisking, and continue whisking until the mixture is emulsified. Add salt and pepper to taste. Cover and chill the dressing until you are ready to use it. Let stand at room temperature for 5 minutes before whisking again and serving.

This dressing will keep for up to 4 days in an airtight container in the refrigerator.

Makes about $^1/_2$ cup

Olive and Herb Vinaigrette

Rich black olives, lots of fresh herbs, and sweet red pepper give this vinaigrette extra character. I love this vinaigrette on a green salad! It also makes a distinctive marinade for any meat or fish.

3 tablespoons white wine vinegar
4 teaspoons Dijon mustard
$^1/_3$ cup extra virgin olive oil
$^1/_3$ cup chopped fresh herbs (basil, chives, tarragon, parsley, mint, etc.)
$^1/_4$ cup finely diced red bell pepper
$^1/_4$ cup pitted and chopped Kalamata or other black olives
Salt and freshly ground pepper

In a small bowl, combine the vinegar and mustard. Whisk to mix well. Slowly add the oil while whisking, and continue whisking until the mixture is emulsified. Whisk in the herbs, bell pepper, olives, and salt and pepper to taste. Cover and chill the dressing until you are ready to use it. Let stand at room temperature for 5 minutes before whisking again and serving.

This dressing will keep for up to 4 days in an airtight container in the refrigerator.

Makes about 1$^1/_4$ cups

Lemon and Caper Vinaigrette

The briny flavor of capers meets the fresh, tart flavor of lemon. This vinaigrette gives salads the sunny flavor of the Mediterranean. As a marinade, it is outstanding with poultry and seafood.

Juice of $1/2$ lemon
2 tablespoons chopped fresh dill, or $3/4$ teaspoon dried
2 tablespoons chopped fresh parsley (preferably flat-leaf)
1 clove garlic, minced
$1/3$ cup plus 1 tablespoon any vegetable oil
Salt and freshly ground pepper
1 tablespoon capers, rinsed and drained

In a small bowl, combine the lemon juice, dill, parsley, and garlic. Whisk to mix well. Slowly add the oil while whisking, and continue whisking until the mixture is emulsified. Or combine the ingredients in a jar and blend with a hand blender. Add salt and pepper to taste. Stir in the capers. Cover and chill the dressing until you are ready to use it. Let stand at room temperature for 5 minutes before whisking again and serving.

This dressing will keep for up to 4 days in an airtight container in the refrigerator.

Makes about 1 cup

Mustard and Parsley Salad Dressing and Marinade

A truly rich blend with a proportion of 4 parts oil to 1 part lemon juice. It is the parsley, however, that carries the day here. This is a lovely dressing for a seafood salad and a lovely marinade for seafood.

> 1 cup chopped fresh parsley (preferably flat-leaf)
> 3 tablespoons freshly squeezed lemon juice
> 1 1/2 tablespoons sugar
> 1/2 teaspoon Dijon mustard
> 1 clove garlic, minced
> 1 teaspoon chopped fresh rosemary
> 3/4 cup extra virgin olive oil
> Salt and freshly ground pepper

In a small bowl, combine the parsley, lemon juice, sugar, mustard, garlic, and rosemary. Whisk to mix well. Slowly add the oil while whisking, and continue whisking until the mixture is emulsified. Or combine the ingredients in a jar and blend with a hand blender. Add salt and pepper to taste. Cover and chill the dressing until you are ready to use it. Let stand at room temperature for 5 minutes before whisking again and serving.

This dressing will keep for up to 4 days in an airtight container in the refrigerator.

Makes about 2 cups

Perfect Pesto Vinaigrette

This is wonderful for a pasta salad and a flavorful marinade for poultry or fish. If you have a mortar and pestle or don't mind doing a lot of chopping by hand, you can make this one without a blender or food processor.

1 cup loosely packed fresh basil leaves
$1/4$ cup freshly grated Parmesan cheese
2 tablespoons white wine vinegar
2 tablespoons freshly squeezed lemon juice
2 tablespoons chopped fresh parsley (preferably flat-leaf)
2 cloves garlic
$1/2$ cup extra virgin olive oil
Salt and freshly ground pepper

In a jar with a hand blender or in a food processor fitted with a steel blade, combine the basil, Parmesan, vinegar, lemon juice, parsley, and garlic. Blend until the herbs are finely chopped. With the motor running, slowly add the oil and continue processing until the oil is fully incorporated into the mixture. Add salt and pepper to taste. Cover and chill the dressing until you are ready to use it. Let stand at room temperature for 5 minutes before mixing again and serving.

This dressing will keep for up to 4 days in an airtight container in the refrigerator.

Makes about 2 cups

Fresh Basil Dijon Vinaigrette

It's always interesting to me how a small change in ingredients can result in a big change in flavor. Here's another basil-based dressing, but the combination of mustard and cider vinegar gives this dressing a tart, spicy flavor.

  1/2 cup cider vinegar
  1/2 cup loosely packed fresh basil leaves
  1/4 cup loosely packed fresh parsley (preferably flat-leaf)
  2 tablespoons Dijon mustard
  2 cloves garlic
  1 cup any vegetable oil
  Salt and freshly ground pepper

In a jar with a hand blender or in a food processor fitted with a steel blade, combine the vinegar, basil, parsley, mustard, and garlic. Blend until finely chopped. With the motor running, slowly add the oil and continue processing until the oil is fully incorporated into the mixture. Add salt and pepper to taste. Cover and chill the dressing until you are ready to use it. Let stand at room temperature for 5 minutes before mixing again and serving.

This dressing will keep for up to 4 days in an airtight container in the refrigerator.

Makes about 2 cups

Lemon Shallot Salad Dressing and Marinade

Shallots, the underused member of the onion family, come in just the right size for flavoring a small batch of salad dressing. The best thing about a shallot, however, is that it has the taste of both onion and garlic. If you don't have a shallot on hand, you can use either onion or garlic as a substitute.

1 small shallot
$^1/_4$ cup freshly squeezed lemon juice
1 to 2 teaspoons sugar
$^1/_3$ cup plus 1 tablespoon any vegetable oil
Salt and freshly ground pepper

In a jar with a hand blender or in a food processor fitted with a steel blade, combine the shallot, lemon juice, and 1 teaspoon sugar. Blend until the shallot is finely chopped. With the motor running, slowly add the oil and continue processing until the oil is fully incorporated into the mixture. Add salt and pepper to taste. Taste and add more sugar if needed. Cover and chill the dressing until you are ready to use it. Let stand at room temperature for 5 minutes before mixing again and serving.

This dressing will keep for up to 4 days in an airtight container in the refrigerator.

Makes about $^3/_4$ cup

Shallot Vinaigrette

For using as a marinade for pork and beef, I particularly like the flavor of dressings made with cider vinegar, like this one.

2 tablespoons cider vinegar
1 small shallot
1 small clove garlic
1 teaspoon Dijon mustard
$1/2$ teaspoon Worcestershire sauce
$1/2$ teaspoon sugar
$3/4$ cup extra virgin olive oil
Salt and freshly ground pepper

In a jar with a hand blender or in a food processor fitted with a steel blade, combine the vinegar, shallot, garlic, mustard, Worcestershire, and sugar. Blend until the shallot and garlic are finely chopped. With the motor running, slowly add the oil and continue processing until the oil is fully incorporated into the mixture. Add salt and pepper to taste. Cover and chill the dressing until you are ready to use it. Let stand at room temperature for 5 minutes before mixing again and serving.

This dressing will keep for up to 4 days in an airtight container in the refrigerator.

Makes about 1 cup

Red Onion and Poppy Seed Salad Dressing and Marinade

This sweet-tart dressing is outstanding on a spinach salad. It also makes a fine marinade for beef. Poppy seeds are one of those special-occasion spices that can go stale in the back of the cupboard; be sure yours taste fresh before using them. Poppy seeds also tend to stick together when packed and need to be broken up with a sifter before adding to this dressing.

> $^1/_3$ cup chopped red onion
> $^1/_4$ cup red wine vinegar
> 1 to 2 tablespoons sugar
> $^1/_2$ cup any vegetable oil
> $^1/_2$ teaspoon poppy seeds
> Salt and freshly ground white pepper

In a small bowl, combine the onion, vinegar, and 1 tablespoon sugar. Whisk to mix well. Slowly add the oil while whisking, and continue whisking until the mixture is emulsified. Sift in the poppy seeds and add salt and pepper to taste. Taste and add more sugar if necessary. Cover and chill the dressing until you are ready to use it. Let stand at room temperature for 5 minutes before whisking again and serving.

This dressing will keep for up to 4 days in an airtight container in the refrigerator.

Makes about $1^1/_4$ cups

Caramelized Onion Vinaigrette

The texture of this dressing is rather thick; a little goes a long way. This makes a flavorful marinade for any meat or fish.

> 3 tablespoons any vegetable oil
> $1/2$ onion, thinly sliced
> 2 to 3 tablespoons balsamic vinegar
> 1 tablespoon honey
> 1 teaspoon Dijon mustard
> Salt and freshly ground pepper

In a small skillet, heat 1 tablespoon of the oil over medium heat. Add the onion and sauté until very soft and golden, about 15 minutes. Let cool. In a small bowl, combine the onion with the remaining 2 tablespoons oil, 2 tablespoons vinegar, honey, and mustard. Taste and add more vinegar if needed. Mix well. Add salt and pepper to taste. Cover and chill the dressing until you are ready to use it. Let stand at room temperature for 5 minutes before mixing again and serving.

This dressing will keep for up to 4 days in an airtight container in the refrigerator.

Makes about $3/4$ cup

Balsamic Vinaigrette

This Italian-style dressing has both honey and balsamic vinegar to contribute a little extra sweetness, which is nicely balanced by the salty Parmesan and the tart lemon and mustard.

2 to 3 tablespoons balsamic vinegar
2 tablespoons honey
1 tablespoon freshly squeezed lemon juice
1 tablespoon Dijon mustard
1 tablespoon chopped fresh basil, or 1 teaspoon dried
$1^1/_2$ teaspoons freshly grated Parmesan cheese
2 cloves garlic, minced
3 tablespoons extra virgin olive oil
Salt and freshly ground pepper

In a small bowl, combine 2 tablespoons of the vinegar, the honey, lemon juice, mustard, basil, Parmesan, and garlic. Mix well. Slowly add the oil while whisking, and continue whisking until the mixture is emulsified. Taste and add more vinegar if necessary. Add salt and pepper to taste. Cover and chill the dressing until you are ready to use it. Let stand at room temperature for 5 minutes before whisking again and serving.

This dressing will keep for up to 4 days in an airtight container in the refrigerator.

Makes about $^3/_4$ cup

Warm Balsamic Vinaigrette

When the warm dressing makes contact with sturdy greens, such as spinach, the salad wilts. This texture change is actually quite pleasant; just don't choose this dressing for a baby lettuce or a delicate mesclun mix. It's wonderful on asparagus, grilled leeks, and other cooked vegetables.

1 tablespoon extra virgin olive oil
3 large shallots, minced
1 clove garlic, minced
2 to 3 tablespoons balsamic vinegar
1 tablespoon Dijon mustard
Salt and freshly ground pepper

In a medium-size skillet, heat the oil over medium heat. Add the shallots and garlic and sauté until soft, about 5 minutes. Add 2 tablespoons of the vinegar, the mustard, and salt and pepper to taste. Mix well. Taste and add more vinegar if necessary. Serve warm.

Makes about ¹/₂ cup

Cowboy Vinaigrette

We call this one Cowboy Vinaigrette at my house because it is so robust in flavor. The horseradish and cayenne give it a pleasant spicy flavor. I love to crumble a little bacon on top of salads dressed with this vinaigrette.

$^1/_3$ cup cider vinegar
2 tablespoons chopped onion
1 tablespoon sugar
1 teaspoon Worcestershire sauce
1 teaspoon prepared horseradish
$^1/_2$ teaspoon Dijon mustard
Pinch of cayenne
$^3/_4$ cup plus 1 tablespoon any vegetable or nut oil
Salt and freshly ground pepper

In a small bowl, combine the vinegar, onion, sugar, Worcestershire, horseradish, mustard, and cayenne. Whisk to mix well. Slowly add the oil while whisking, and continue whisking until the mixture is emulsified. Add salt and pepper to taste. Cover and chill the dressing until you are ready to use it. Let stand at room temperature for 5 minutes before whisking again and serving.

This dressing will keep for up to 7 days in an airtight container in the refrigerator.

Makes about 1$^1/_3$ cups

Humble Honey Salad Dressing and Marinade

You'll notice that this recipe calls for celery leaves, meaning the leaves at the top of the celery stalk. They add a wonderful fresh flavor to a dressing.

> $^1/_3$ cup cider vinegar
> $^1/_4$ to $^1/_3$ cup honey
> 1 to 2 tablespoons sugar
> 1 tablespoon finely chopped red onion
> 1 teaspoon Dijon mustard
> $^1/_2$ teaspoon finely chopped celery leaves
> $^3/_4$ cup any vegetable or nut oil
> Salt and freshly ground pepper

In a small bowl, combine the vinegar, $^1/_4$ cup honey, 1 tablespoon sugar, the onion, mustard, and celery leaves. Whisk to mix well. Slowly add the oil while whisking, and continue whisking until the mixture is emulsified. Add salt and pepper to taste. Check to see if there is enough honey and sugar in the dressing and add more if needed. Cover and chill the dressing until you are ready to use it. Let stand at room temperature for 5 minutes before whisking again and serving.

This dressing will keep for up to 7 days in an airtight container in the refrigerator.

Makes about 1$^3/_4$ cups

Orange Sunshine Salad Dressing and Marinade

This really does taste like sunshine! Try it as a marinade for duck or any poultry. It can also be served as a dressing for a warm duck salad. You can use any oil in the dressing, but I prefer it with extra virgin olive oil. The rice vinegar is less tart than other vinegars; you can buy it wherever Asian foods are sold.

 $^1/_4$ cup freshly squeezed orange juice
 $^1/_4$ cup rice vinegar
 2 tablespoons freshly squeezed lemon juice
 1 tablespoon sugar
 1 teaspoon Dijon mustard
 $^1/_4$ cup any vegetable or nut oil
 Salt and freshly ground pepper

In a small bowl, combine the orange juice, vinegar, lemon juice, sugar, and mustard. Whisk to mix well. Slowly add the oil while whisking, and continue whisking until the mixture is emulsified. Add salt and pepper to taste. Cover and chill the dressing until you are ready to use it. Let stand at room temperature for 5 minutes before whisking again and serving.

This dressing will keep for up to 7 days in an airtight container in the refrigerator.

Makes about 1 cup

Lime Vinaigrette

This is a great fajita marinade. It is also excellent as a marinade for seafood.

3 tablespoons freshly squeezed lime juice
2 tablespoons honey
1 tablespoon cider vinegar
$1/3$ cup any vegetable oil
3 tablespoons chopped fresh cilantro
2 tablespoons finely chopped green onions, white part only
$1/2$ teaspoon grated lime zest
Salt and freshly ground pepper

In a small bowl, combine the lime juice, honey, and vinegar. Whisk to mix well. Slowly add the oil while whisking, and continue whisking until the mixture is emulsified. Stir in the cilantro, green onions, and zest. Add salt and pepper to taste. Cover and chill the dressing until you are ready to use it. Let stand at room temperature for 5 minutes before whisking again and serving.

This dressing will keep for up to 2 days in an airtight container in the refrigerator.

Makes about 1 cup

Great Grapefruit-Honey Salad Dressing and Marinade

This is one of my all-time favorites. I like to make a salad using Boston lettuce, sections of a pink grapefruit, thinly sliced red onions, and sugared or toasted almonds or pecans.

> 3 tablespoons cider vinegar
> 3 tablespoons freshly squeezed grapefruit juice
> 2 tablespoons honey
> 1 clove garlic, minced
> Pinch of cayenne
> $1/4$ cup any vegetable oil
> Salt and freshly ground pepper

In a small bowl, combine the vinegar, grapefruit juice, honey, garlic, and cayenne. Whisk to mix well. Slowly add the oil while whisking, and continue whisking until the mixture is emulsified. Add salt and pepper to taste. Cover and chill the dressing until you are ready to use it. Let stand at room temperature for 5 minutes before whisking again and serving.

This dressing will keep for up to 4 days in an airtight container in the refrigerator.

Makes about $3/4$ cup

Spicy Green Chile Dressing and Marinade

This wonderful dressing is light on oil, but rich with flavor. It makes an excellent barbecue sauce for meat and chicken. I also like it on a taco salad.

1 (4-ounce) can green chiles, drained and diced
$^1/_2$ cup cider vinegar
1 tomato, peeled, seeded, and chopped (see note)
1 tablespoon any vegetable oil
1 tablespoon chopped fresh parsley (preferably flat-leaf)
2 cloves garlic
2 teaspoons sugar
Salt and freshly ground pepper

In a jar with a hand blender or in a food processor or blender, combine all the ingredients, adding salt and pepper to taste. Process to mix. Cover and chill the dressing until you are ready to use it. Let stand at room temperature for 5 minutes before mixing again and serving.

This dressing will keep for up to 2 weeks in an airtight container in the refrigerator.

Note: To remove the skin from tomatoes, dip them in boiling water for 30 seconds, then quickly run cold water over them to stop the cooking process; the skins should just slip off. To seed a tomato, cut it in half horizontally and gently squeeze.

Makes about 1 cup

Tangy Tomato Dressing and Marinade

This is a great dressing to use with a taco salad.

$^1/_2$ cup loosely packed fresh cilantro leaves
2 cloves garlic
1 jalapeño, seeded and chopped
1 large tomato, peeled, seeded, and chopped
  (see note page 35)
3 tablespoons red wine vinegar
2 tablespoons freshly squeezed lemon juice
1 teaspoon ground cumin
$^1/_2$ teaspoon dried oregano
10 tablespoons any vegetable oil
Salt and freshly ground pepper

In a jar with a hand blender or in a food processor fitted with a steel blade, combine the cilantro, garlic, and jalapeño. Process until chopped. Add the tomato, vinegar, lemon juice, cumin, and oregano and process to blend well. Slowly add the oil, processing until the mixture is emulsified. Add salt and pepper to taste. Cover and chill. Let the dressing stand at room temperature for 5 minutes before mixing again and serving.

This dressing will keep for up to 4 days in an airtight container in the refrigerator.

Makes about 1$^1/_2$ cups

Catalina Salad Dressing

The origins of this salad dressing are obscure, but its popularity is unquestioned. This is a family favorite. It makes an excellent, all-purpose marinade.

$^1\!/_3$ cup ketchup
$^1\!/_4$ to $^1\!/_3$ cup sugar
$^1\!/_4$ cup white wine vinegar
1 small onion, chopped
$^3\!/_4$ cup any vegetable oil
Salt and freshly ground pepper

In a jar with a hand blender or in a food processor fitted with a steel blade, combine the ketchup, $^1\!/_4$ cup sugar, the vinegar, and onion. Process until the onion is finely chopped. Slowly add the oil, processing until the mixture is emulsified. Add salt and pepper to taste. Taste and add more sugar if necessary. Cover and chill the dressing until you are ready to use it. Let stand at room temperature for 5 minutes before mixing again and serving.

This dressing will keep for up to 2 weeks in an airtight container in the refrigerator.

Makes about 1 cup

Fiesta Salad Dressing

Add leftover chicken or turkey to your greens, dress with this salad dressing, and enjoy a hearty lunch salad or a light main course.

2$^{1}/_{2}$ tablespoons cider vinegar

1 tablespoon mild salsa

1 small clove garlic

1 teaspoon chopped fresh oregano, or $^{1}/_{8}$ teaspoon dried

1 teaspoon chopped fresh cilantro

$^{1}/_{8}$ teaspoon ground cumin

$^{1}/_{8}$ teaspoon seasoning salt

$^{1}/_{8}$ teaspoon freshly ground pepper

$^{1}/_{4}$ cup any vegetable oil

In a jar with a hand blender or in a food processor fitted with a steel blade, combine the vinegar, salsa, garlic, oregano, cilantro, cumin, salt, and pepper. Process until the garlic is finely shopped. Slowly add the oil, processing until the mixture is emulsified. Cover and chill the dressing until you are ready to use it. Let stand at room temperature for 5 minutes before mixing again and serving.

This dressing will keep for up to 5 days in an airtight container in the refrigerator.

Makes about $^{1}/_{2}$ cup

Wasabi Vinaigrette

Wasabi is a hot Japanese condiment that is traditionally used in sushi. You may have to adjust the amount you use as different brands have different levels of heat.

> 2 tablespoons cider vinegar
> 1 tablespoon freshly squeezed lemon juice
> 1 tablespoon wasabi paste or powder
> 2 cloves garlic
> 1 teaspoon sugar
> $1/4$ cup any vegetable or nut oil
> 2 tablespoons chopped fresh cilantro
> 1 teaspoon chopped fresh thyme, or $1/2$ teaspoon dried
> Salt and freshly ground pepper

In a jar with a hand blender or in a food processor fitted with a steel blade, combine the vinegar, lemon juice, wasabi, garlic, and sugar. Process until the garlic is finely chopped. Slowly add the oil, processing until the mixture is emulsified. Stir in the cilantro, thyme, and salt and pepper to taste. Cover and chill the dressing until you are ready to use it. Let stand at room temperature for 5 minutes before mixing again and serving.

This dressing will keep for up to 4 days in an airtight container in the refrigerator.

Makes about $3/4$ cup

Sunny Dried Tomato Vinaigrette

Use sun-dried tomatoes packed in oil. They are softer and process easier.

> 1/4 cup chopped oil-packed sun-dried tomatoes
> 1/4 cup roasted, peeled, seeded, and chopped red bell
>   pepper (see note)
> 2 tablespoons white wine vinegar
> 2 tablespoons balsamic vinegar
> 2 tablespoons chopped fresh parsley (preferably flat-leaf)
> 1 clove garlic
> 1/3 cup any vegetable oil
> Salt and freshly ground pepper

In a jar with a hand blender or in a food processor fitted with a steel blade, combine the tomatoes, bell pepper, wine and balsamic vinegars, parsley, and garlic. Process until the garlic and tomatoes are very finely chopped. Slowly add the oil, processing until the mixture is emulsified. Add salt and pepper to taste. Cover and chill the dressing until you are ready to use it. Let stand at room temperature for 5 minutes before mixing again and serving.

This dressing will keep for up to 1 week in an airtight container in the refrigerator.

Note: To roast bell peppers, place over a gas flame or under a broiler and roast, turning frequently, until charred and blistered all over. Transfer to a paper or plastic bag, seal, and set aside to steam for 10 minutes. Carefully peel the peppers, using a dry paper towel to wipe away any stubborn, charred skin. Never scrub roasted peppers under running water as it removes their delicious, smoky flavor.

Makes about 1 cup

Thai Dressing and Marinade

This dressing gets quite a bit of fire from crushed red pepper flakes—use less if you don't like hot foods. This makes an excellent marinade for poultry and seafood.

6 tablespoons freshly squeezed lime juice
$^1/_4$ cup any vegetable oil
$^1/_4$ cup soy sauce
3 cloves garlic, minced
$1^1/_4$ tablespoons smooth peanut butter
1 tablespoon crushed red pepper flakes
Salt and freshly ground pepper

Combine all the ingredients in a bowl or jar adding salt and pepper to taste, and stir or shake to blend well. Cover and chill the dressing until you are ready to use it. Let stand at room temperature for 5 minutes before stirring or shaking again and serving.

This dressing will keep for up to 1 week in an airtight container in the refrigerator.

Makes about 1 cup

Tahini Dressing and Marinade

If you haven't yet enjoyed the flavor of tahini in a Middle Eastern dish, this dressing is a good way to begin. Tahini is a paste made of raw sesame seeds, similar in consistency to peanut butter.

$^1/_3$ cup any vegetable oil
3 tablespoons freshly squeezed lemon juice
2 tablespoons tahini
1 clove garlic, minced
Dash of Tabasco sauce
Salt and freshly ground pepper

Combine all the ingredients in a bowl or jar, adding salt and pepper to taste. Stir or shake to blend well. Cover and chill the dressing until you are ready to use it. Serve at room temperature.

This dressing will keep for up to 2 weeks in an airtight container in the refrigerator.

Makes about $^2/_3$ cup

Seedy Cilantro Salad Dressing and Marinade

Cilantro is an herb that you either love or hate. It has a distinctive musky flavor. It is used extensively in the cooking of Mexico and Southeast Asia. This dressing is Asian in character.

$1/4$ cup toasted sesame seeds (see note)
3 tablespoons rice vinegar
$2^{1}/_{2}$ tablespoons freshly squeezed lemon juice
1 tablespoon sake or dry sherry
1 tablespoon soy sauce
1 clove garlic
1 cup loosely packed fresh cilantro leaves
2 tablespoons toasted sesame oil
$1/_{3}$ cup peanut oil
Salt and freshly ground pepper

In a jar with a hand blender or in a food processor fitted with a steel blade, combine the sesame seeds, vinegar, lemon juice, sake, soy sauce, and garlic. Process until the garlic is finely chopped. Add the cilantro and sesame oil and blend again. Slowly add the peanut oil, processing until the mixture is emulsified. Stir in the salt and pepper to taste. Cover and chill the dressing until you are ready to use it. Let stand at room temperature for 5 minutes before mixing again and serving.

This dressing will keep for up to 2 days in an airtight container in the refrigerator.

Note: To toast sesame seeds, place the seeds in a dry skillet over medium heat and cook, stirring constantly for about 3 minutes, until golden and fragrant.

Makes about 1 1/3 cups

Spinach Salad Dressing

This is a classic dressing. Toss with spinach and top the salad with crumbled bacon and pepper to taste.

    1 tablespoon warm bacon drippings
    1 small onion, minced
    2 tablespoons dry sherry
    2 tablespoons honey

Combine the bacon drippings, onion, sherry, and honey in a bowl or jar and stir or shake to blend well. Serve at once.

Makes about $^1/_3$ cup

Real Roquefort Dressing

Roquefort is one of the oldest and best-loved cheeses in the world. A creamy blue cheese made from sheep's milk, it has been enjoyed since Roman times. The name "Roquefort" is protected by law to mean only blue cheese that is aged in the caverns of Mount Combalou near the village of Roquefort. If you want the real stuff, be sure the package has a red sheep on the wrapper.

1/4 cup rice vinegar
2 tablespoons chopped fresh thyme, or 3/4 teaspoon dried
1 teaspoon Dijon mustard
1 clove garlic
1/2 cup extra virgin olive oil
1/4 cup crumbled Roquefort cheese
Salt and freshly ground pepper

In a jar with a hand blender or in a food processor fitted with a steel blade, combine the vinegar, thyme, mustard, and garlic. Blend until the garlic is finely chopped. Slowly add the oil, processing until the mixture is emulsified. Stir in the cheese and salt and pepper to taste. Cover and chill the dressing until you are ready to use it. Let stand at room temperature for 5 minutes before mixing again and serving.

This dressing will keep for up to 5 days in an airtight container in the refrigerator.

Makes about 1 cup

Italian Parmesan Salad Dressing

I like the combination of oil, vinegar, and cheese in this dressing.

$1/3$ cup balsamic vinegar
$1/4$ cup freshly grated Parmesan cheese
$1^1/2$ tablespoons freshly squeezed lemon juice
2 green onions, green part only, chopped
2 teaspoons Worcestershire sauce
2 cloves garlic
1 tablespoon chopped fresh oregano, or 1 teaspoon dried
$1/2$ cup plus 1 tablespoon olive oil
Dash of Tabasco sauce
Salt and freshly ground pepper

In a jar with a hand blender or in a food processor fitted with a steel blade, combine the vinegar, Parmesan, lemon juice, green onions, Worcestershire, garlic, and oregano. Blend until the garlic and oregano are finely chopped. Slowly add the oil, processing until the mixture is emulsified. Stir in the Tabasco and salt and pepper to taste. Cover and chill the dressing until you are ready to use it. Let stand at room temperature for 5 minutes before mixing again and serving.

This dressing will keep for up to 7 days in an airtight container in the refrigerator.

Makes about $1^1/2$ cups

Gorgonzola Salad Dressing

Made from cow's milk, Gorgonzola is rich, creamy, and fairly pungent. A little goes a long way in flavoring a dressing.

- $1/2$ cup crumbled Gorgonzola cheese
- $1/3$ cup any vegetable oil
- 2 tablespoons freshly squeezed lemon juice
- 2 tablespoons white wine vinegar
- 2 tablespoons sour cream
- 1 teaspoon Dijon mustard
- 1 teaspoon sugar
- 1 clove garlic
- Salt and freshly ground pepper

In a jar with a hand blender or in a food processor fitted with a steel blade, combine all the ingredients, adding salt and pepper to taste. Blend until well mixed. Cover and chill the dressing until you are ready to use it. Let stand at room temperature for 5 minutes before mixing again and serving.

This dressing will keep for up to 4 days in an airtight container in the refrigerator.

Makes about $1^1/4$ cups

Variation: Instead of the Gorgonzola, experiment with Roquefort, feta, or Romano cheese.

Caesar Salad Dressing #1

A wooden salad bowl is best for making this Caesar salad. To serve, add romaine lettuce to the dressing in the bowl, toss well, add croutons, and sprinkle with additional Parmesan cheese.

2 cloves garlic, minced
2 teaspoons anchovy paste
1 tablespoon freshly grated Parmesan cheese
$3/4$ teaspoon Dijon mustard
$1/2$ teaspoon Worcestershire sauce
1 egg yolk (see pages 7 to 9)
3 tablespoons freshly squeezed lemon juice
1 tablespoon red wine vinegar
$1/3$ cup plus 1 tablespoon extra virgin olive oil
Salt and freshly ground pepper

In a large salad bowl, combine the garlic and anchovy paste. Mash together well. Add the Parmesan, mustard, and Worcestershire and mix well. Then add the egg, lemon juice, and vinegar. Add the oil and mix well. Add salt and pepper to taste. Serve immediately.

Makes about 1 cup

Caesar Salad Dressing #2

This dressing is just a more garlicky variation of #1. It's the closest to a traditional Caesar dressing.

> 1 egg (see pages 7 to 9)
> $^1/_4$ cup freshly squeezed lemon juice
> 3 cloves garlic
> 1 tablespoon anchovy paste
> $^1/_2$ cup extra virgin olive oil
> $^1/_4$ cup freshly grated Parmesan cheese
> Freshly ground pepper

In a jar with a hand blender or in a food processor fitted with a steel blade, combine the egg, lemon juice, garlic, and anchovy paste. Blend until the garlic is finely chopped. Slowly add the oil, processing until the mixture is emulsified. Stir in the Parmesan cheese and pepper to taste. Serve at once.

Makes about 1 cup

Sweet-and-Sour Salad Dressing

This is one of my all-time favorites—simple ingredients, simply delicious. The egg really adds to the flavor, so don't leave it out if you don't have to.

> 1 egg yolk (see pages 7 to 9)
> $^1/_4$ cup sugar
> 3 tablespoons red wine vinegar
> Juice of $^1/_2$ lemon
> 1 teaspoon dry mustard
> $^1/_2$ teaspoon white pepper
> $^1/_2$ cup any vegetable oil
> Salt

In a jar with a hand blender or in a food processor fitted with a steel blade, combine the egg, sugar, vinegar, lemon juice, mustard, and pepper. Blend until well mixed. Slowly add the oil, processing until the mixture is emulsified. Stir in salt to taste. Serve at once.

Makes about 1 $^1/_2$ cups

Old World Dressing

This one was my Nana's tried and true. I know it sounds odd and a bit old-fashioned, but try it. You'll love it!

$^1/_4$ cup red wine vinegar
2 tablespoons whipping cream
$1^1/_2$ teaspoons Dijon mustard
$1^1/_2$ teaspoons Worcestershire sauce
1 egg yolk (see pages 7 to 9)
1 teaspoon A-1 steak sauce
2 cloves garlic
$^2/_3$ cup any vegetable oil
Salt and freshly ground pepper

In a jar with a hand blender or in a food processor fitted with a steel blade, combine the vinegar, cream, mustard, Worcestershire, egg, steak sauce, and garlic. Blend until the garlic is finely chopped. Slowly add the oil, processing until the mixture is emulsified. Stir in the salt and pepper to taste. Serve at once.

Makes about 1 cup

Salad Dressings and Marinades
Made with Fruits and Vegetables

Really Raspberry Vinaigrette

Raspberry vinaigrettes are extremely popular, and with good reason; their flavor works particularly well with green salads that include tart and tangy lettuces and greens.

  1 cup fresh raspberries
  1 shallot, chopped
  $^1/_2$ cup white wine vinegar
  1 to 2 tablespoons honey
  1 tablespoon walnut or any vegetable oil
  Salt and freshly ground pepper

In a jar with a hand blender or in a food processor fitted with a steel blade, puree the raspberries. Strain, reserving the juice and discarding the seeds and pulp. Return the raspberry juice to the jar or bowl and combine with the shallot, vinegar, 1 tablespoon honey, oil, and salt and pepper to taste. Blend to mix. Cover and chill the dressing until you are ready to use it. Let stand at room temperature for 5 minutes before mixing again and serving. Taste the dressing to make sure the sweet-sour balance is correct. If you want the vinaigrette to be sweeter, add the remaining 1 tablespoon honey.

This dressing will keep for up to 1 week in an airtight container in the refrigerator.

Makes about 1 $^1/_2$ cups

Blueberry Vinaigrette

Raspberries have already caught the attention of salad makers, but blueberries can also contribute their unique summery flavor in dressings and marinades.

$^1/_3$ cup fresh blueberries
2 tablespoons cider vinegar
1 tablespoon freshly squeezed lemon juice
1 tablespoon minced red onion
1 teaspoon sugar
$^1/_2$ teaspoon dry mustard
$^1/_4$ cup any vegetable or nut oil
Salt and freshly ground pepper

In a jar with a hand blender or in a food processor fitted with a steel blade, combine the blueberries, vinegar, lemon juice, onion, sugar, and mustard. Blend until the blueberries are pureed. Strain, discarding the seeds and skin. Return the blueberry juice to the jar or bowl. With the motor running, slowly add the oil and continue processing until the oil is fully incorporated into the mixture. Add salt and pepper to taste. Cover and chill the dressing until you are ready to use it. Let stand at room temperature for 5 minutes before mixing again and serving.

This dressing will keep for up to 4 days in an airtight container in the refrigerator.

Makes about $^3/_4$ cup

Strawberry Surprise

The surprise is how wonderful fruity dressings go with green salads. It is also lovely on a grilled chicken breast bedded down on salad greens.

9 fresh strawberries
$1/3$ cup any vegetable oil
$1/4$ cup honey
2 tablespoons freshly squeezed grapefruit juice
2 tablespoons cider vinegar
1 teaspoon dry mustard
Salt and freshly ground pepper

In a jar with a hand blender or in a food processor fitted with a steel blade, combine all the ingredients, adding salt and pepper to taste. Blend until well mixed. Cover and chill the dressing until you are ready to use it. Let stand at room temperature for 5 minutes before mixing again and serving.

This dressing will keep for up to 2 days in an airtight container in the refrigerator.

Makes about 1 cup

Papa's Papaya Dressing and Marinade

The only challenging part of this recipe is choosing a ripe papaya. Look for richly colored fruit that gives slightly to the touch. If it is still a little green, store it overnight in a paper bag. Refrigerate perfectly ripe fruit and use it quickly.

1 papaya, peeled, seeded, and chopped
3 tablespoons chopped red onion
3 tablespoons white wine vinegar
1 tablespoon any vegetable oil
1 tablespoon honey
1 tablespoon chopped fresh sage, or $1/4$ teaspoon dried
Salt and freshly ground pepper

In a jar with a hand blender or in a food processor fitted with a steel blade, combine all the ingredients, adding salt and pepper to taste. Blend until well mixed. Cover and chill the dressing until you are ready to use it. Let stand at room temperature for 5 minutes before mixing again and serving.

This dressing will keep for up to 2 days in an airtight container in the refrigerator.

Makes about 1 cup

My Mango Salad Dressing and Marinade

You'll taste the tropics in this lovely dressing. It makes an excellent marinade for poultry and seafood. If your mango lacks flavor, add 1 tablespoon honey to this dressing. Notice this contains no oil at all.

1 mango peeled, seeded, and chopped
$1/4$ cup freshly squeezed orange juice
3 tablespoons freshly squeezed lemon juice
3 tablespoons cider vinegar
1 teaspoon ground ginger
$1/2$ teaspoon grated orange zest
Salt and freshly ground pepper
2 tablespoons chopped fresh cilantro

In a jar with a hand blender or in a food processor fitted with a steel blade, combine the mango, orange juice, lemon juice, vinegar, ginger, orange zest, and salt and pepper to taste. Blend until well mixed. Stir in the cilantro. Cover and chill the dressing until you are ready to use it. Let stand at room temperature for 5 minutes before mixing again and serving.

This dressing will keep for up to 2 days in an airtight container in the refrigerator.

Makes about $1^3/4$ cups

Pear-Apple Surprise

This is wonderful as a dressing for finely shredded green cabbage or shredded romaine lettuce. My favorite combination of fruit varieties in this recipe is a Granny Smith apple with a Comice pear.

> 1 apple, peeled and diced
> 1 pear, peeled and diced
> 1 small red onion, diced
> 3 tablespoons cider vinegar
> 1 tablespoon any vegetable oil
> 1 tablespoon chopped fresh parsley (preferably flat-leaf)
> 2 tablespoons apple cider
> Pinch of salt

Combine all the ingredients in a medium-size bowl and stir well. Cover and chill the dressing until you are ready to use it. This is best served on the day it is made.

Makes about 1 1/2 cups

Peach and Pepper Dressing

This fruity mix is a treat served over grilled fish. As a dressing, it's fine over a mix of baby lettuce leaves. Note that it contains only 1 teaspoon of oil.

2 peaches, peeled and diced
1 to 2 jalapeños, seeded and diced
3 tablespoons finely chopped green onions, white part only
2 tablespoons finely chopped red bell pepper
1 tablespoon freshly squeezed lime juice
1 tablespoon chopped fresh parsley (preferably flat-leaf)
1 tablespoon chopped fresh cilantro
1 teaspoon extra virgin olive oil
$^1/_2$ teaspoon ground cumin
Salt and freshly ground pepper

Combine all the ingredients in a medium-size bowl, adding salt and pepper to taste. Stir well. Cover and chill the dressing until you are ready to use it. This is best served on the day it is made.

Makes about 1³/₄ cups

Roasted Pepper Salad Dressing and Marinade

This is a wonderful dressing for roasted vegetables—even lettuce. Try roasting a head of iceburg or romaine lettuce, halved lengthwise, cut side down, in a 425° F degree oven for 5 minutes on each side.

> 1 red, yellow, or green bell pepper, roasted, peeled, seeded, and chopped (see note page 40)
> 2 tablespoons white wine vinegar
> 1 tablespoon freshly squeezed lemon juice
> 2 cloves garlic
> 1 tablespoon chopped fresh chives
> Salt and freshly ground pepper

In a jar with a hand blender or in a food processor fitted with a steel blade, combine the pepper, vinegar, lemon juice, and garlic. Process until the pepper and garlic are well chopped. Stir in the chives and salt and pepper to taste. Cover and chill the dressing until you are ready to use it. Let stand at room temperature for 5 minutes before mixing again and serving.

This dressing will keep for up to 4 days in an airtight container in the refrigerator.

Makes about ¹/₂ cup

Mighty Mint Dressing

This is a great dressing for fruit salad. Notice that it doesn't contain any oil.

1 1/2 cups loosely packed fresh cilantro leaves
1/4 cup cider vinegar
1/4 cup honey
2 tablespoons chopped fresh mint
1 tablespoon grated fresh ginger
1 jalapeño, seeded
Salt

In a jar with a hand blender or in a food processor fitted with a steel blade, combine all the ingredients, adding salt to taste. Blend until well chopped. Cover and chill the dressing until you are ready to use it. Let stand at room temperature for 5 minutes before mixing again and serving.

This dressing will keep for up to 2 days in an airtight container in the refrigerator.

Makes about 2 cups

Bombay Dressing

This is a sweet-and-sour dressing that works well with spicy greens or salads with peppers and other bold vegetables.

1/3 cup coarsely chopped carrot
1/3 cup coarsely chopped celery
2 tablespoons chopped onion
6 tablespoons sugar
6 tablespoons any vegetable oil
1/4 cup cider vinegar
1/4 teaspoon seasoning salt
Freshly ground pepper

In a jar with a hand blender or in a food processor fitted with a steel blade, combine all the ingredients, including pepper to taste. Process until the vegetables are finely chopped. Cover and chill the dressing until you are ready to use it. Let stand at room temperature for 5 minutes before mixing again and serving.

This dressing will keep for up to 1 week in an airtight container in the refrigerator.

Makes about 1 cup

Warm and Wonderful Mushroom Dressing

In ancient Egypt, mushrooms were called "sons of Gods" sent to earth on thunderbolts because of their mysterious habit of appearing after a rain storm. For a more exotic flavor, chanterelle or shiitake mushrooms can replace half of the white mushrooms in this recipe.

> 3 tablespoons any vegetable or nut oil
> 3 leeks, white part only, thinly sliced
> $^1/_2$ pound button mushrooms, sliced
> 1 clove garlic, minced
> 2 tablespoons chopped fresh parsley (preferably flat-leaf)
> 1 tablespoon freshly squeezed lemon juice
> 1 tablespoon dry sherry
> 1 teaspoon Dijon mustard
> 1 teaspoon red wine vinegar
> Salt and freshly ground pepper

Heat the oil in a large skillet over medium-high heat. Add the leeks and mushrooms and sauté for 5 minutes, or until vegetables have sweated but not yet browned. Add the garlic and sauté for 2 minutes more. Remove from the heat and stir in the parsley, lemon juice, sherry, mustard, vinegar, and salt and pepper to taste. Serve immediately.

Makes about 1$^1/_4$ cups

Lemon Avocado Dressing

This creamy lemon dressing is a refreshing change of pace. Try it on fruit or green salads or on coleslaw.

   1 avocado, peeled, pitted, and mashed
   $1/4$ cup water
   2 tablespoons sour cream (low-fat or nonfat is acceptable)
   2 tablespoons freshly squeezed lemon juice
   1 tablespoon chopped fresh dill
   2 teaspoons any vegetable or nut oil
   1 clove garlic
   1 teaspoon honey
   $1/2$ teaspoon seasoning salt

In a jar with a hand blender or in a food processor fitted with a steel blade, combine all the ingredients and process until well mixed. Cover and chill the dressing until you are ready to use it. Let stand at room temperature for 5 minutes before serving.

This dressing will keep for up to 2 days in an airtight container in the refrigerator.

Makes about 1 cup

Creamy Salad Dressings

Flying R Ranch Dressing

Ranch dressings are buttermilk dressings, usually flavored with onion and garlic and other seasonings. The original ranch dressing is said to have been created by the Henson family, owners of Hidden Valley Ranch near Santa Barbara, California. They began selling their dressing as a dry mix shortly after World War II. This is my version.

$^1/_3$ cup buttermilk
1 tablespoon cider vinegar
1 tablespoon apple juice or cider
1 tablespoon freshly squeezed lemon juice
1 tablespoon sugar
1 clove garlic
1 green onion, white part only, chopped
1 tablespoon chopped fresh thyme, or $^1/_4$ teaspoon dried
1 tablespoon chopped fresh oregano, or $^1/_4$ teaspoon dried
1 egg yolk (see pages 7 to 9)
$^1/_3$ cup any vegetable oil
Salt and freshly ground pepper

In a jar with a hand blender or in a food processor fitted with a steel blade, combine the buttermilk, vinegar, apple juice, lemon juice, sugar, garlic, green onion, thyme, oregano, and egg yolk. Blend until the garlic, green onion, and herbs are finely chopped. With the motor running, slowly add the oil and continue processing until the oil is fully incorporated into the mixture. Add salt and pepper to taste. Cover and chill the dressing until you are ready to use it. Let stand at room temperature for 5 minutes before mixing again and serving.

This dressing is best served the day it is made.

Makes about 1 1/4 cups

Rosy Buttermilk Salad Dressing

With the addition of ketchup, this buttermilk dressing tastes like a cross between a ranch dressing and a Thousand Island–type dressing.

$^3/_4$ cup mayonnaise (reduced-fat is acceptable)
$^1/_3$ cup plus 1 tablespoon buttermilk
$^1/_3$ cup plus 1 tablespoon ketchup
2 cloves garlic, minced
1 teaspoon Worcestershire sauce
1 teaspoon hot paprika
Salt and freshly ground pepper

Combine all the ingredients in a small bowl or jar, adding salt and pepper to taste. Stir or whisk well to combine. Cover and chill the dressing until you are ready to use it. Let stand at room temperature for 5 minutes before mixing again and serving.

This dressing will keep for up to 5 days in an airtight container in the refrigerator.

Makes about 1 $^1/_2$ cups

Creamy Winter Special Salad Dressing

This is a wonderful, bold dressing perfect for the holidays. Sprinkle pomegranate seeds on top of the salad for a sweet and nutty flavor.

$1/2$ cup mayonnaise (reduced-fat is acceptable)
6 tablespoons buttermilk
2 tablespoons cider vinegar
1 shallot, minced
2 cloves garlic, minced
1 tablespoon chopped fresh basil, or $3/4$ teaspoon dried
1 tablespoon chopped fresh thyme, or $3/4$ teaspoon dried
Salt and freshly ground pepper

In a small bowl or jar, combine all the ingredients, adding salt and pepper to taste. Stir or shake to combine. Cover and chill the dressing until you are ready to use it. Let stand at room temperature for 5 minutes before mixing again and serving.

This dressing will keep for up to 5 days in an airtight container in the refrigerator.

Makes about 1 1/4 cups

Montana Herb Dressing

Horseradish and mustard give this ranch-style dressing a lot of zip. If you use nonfat buttermilk and yogurt, you will have a very healthy, low-fat dressing. It also makes a great dip for vegetables.

   $1/2$ cup plain yogurt
   $1/2$ cup mayonnaise (reduced-fat is acceptable)
   $1/4$ cup buttermilk
   1 tablespoon Dijon mustard
   1 tablespoon prepared horseradish
   1 tablespoon chopped fresh parsley (preferably flat-leaf)
   1 tablespoon chopped fresh dill, or $1/2$ teaspoon dried
   Pinch of celery salt
   Freshly ground pepper

In a small bowl or jar, combine all the ingredients, adding pepper to taste. Stir or shake to combine. Cover and chill the dressing until you are ready to use it. Let stand at room temperature for 5 minutes before mixing again and serving.

This dressing will keep for up to 5 days in an airtight container in the refrigerator.

Makes about $1^1/_2$ cups

Russian Dressing

There's no finer spread for a roast beef or grilled Reuben sandwich than this homemade dressing.

$1/3$ cup mayonnaise (reduced-fat is acceptable)
2 tablespoons finely chopped sweet gherkins
1 tablespoon finely chopped onion
1 tablespoon ketchup
$1/2$ teaspoon prepared horseradish
Dash of Worcestershire sauce
Freshly ground pepper

Combine all the ingredients in a small bowl or jar, adding pepper to taste. Stir well to combine. Cover and chill the dressing until you are ready to use it. Let stand at room temperature for 5 minutes before serving.

This dressing will keep for up to 2 weeks in an airtight container in the refrigerator.

Makes about $1/2$ cup

Thousand Island Dressing

So good, and so much better than the bottled type.

   $1/3$ cup mayonnaise (reduced-fat is acceptable)
   $1/3$ cup sour cream (low-fat or nonfat is acceptable)
   $1/4$ cup freshly squeezed lemon juice
   $1/4$ cup chili sauce or ketchup
   $1/4$ cup finely chopped green bell pepper
   2 tablespoons finely chopped onion
   1 tablespoon any vegetable oil
   1 tablespoon chopped fresh parsley (preferably flat-leaf)
   Pinch of cayenne
   Pinch of salt

Combine all the ingredients in a small bowl or jar. Stir well to combine. Cover and chill the dressing until you are ready to use it. Let stand at room temperature for 5 minutes before serving.

This dressing will keep for up to 2 weeks in an airtight container in the refrigerator.

Makes about $1^2/3$ cups

Low-Cal Thousand Island Dressing

If you are trying to avoid fat, consider this version of Thousand Island dressing.

$1/2$ cup low-fat cottage cheese
5 tablespoons tomato juice
3 tablespoons milk
$1^1/2$ teaspoons sugar
2 tablespoons finely chopped onion
2 tablespoons finely chopped green bell pepper
1 tablespoon finely chopped dill pickle
Salt and freshly ground pepper

In a jar with a hand blender or in a food processor fitted with a steel blade, combine the cottage cheese, tomato juice, milk, and sugar. Blend until smooth. Stir in the onion, bell pepper, pickle, and salt and pepper to taste. Cover and chill the dressing until you are ready to use it. Let stand at room temperature for 5 minutes before mixing again and serving.

This dressing will keep for up to 4 days in an airtight container in the refrigerator.

Makes about $3/4$ cup

Tangy Garlic Salad Dressing

Garlic can be mild, like the white kind, or strong, like the rose-colored variety. Garlic should be firm and crisp. The fresher the garlic, the milder the taste.

10 tablespoons mayonnaise (reduced-fat is acceptable)
3 tablespoons cider vinegar
3 tablespoons chopped fresh parsley (preferably flat-leaf)
2 tablespoons Dijon mustard
2 tablespoons ketchup
2 cloves garlic
Pinch of cayenne
Salt and freshly ground pepper

In a jar with a hand blender or in a food processor fitted with a steel blade, combine all the ingredients, adding salt and pepper to taste. Process to blend well. Cover and chill the dressing until you are ready to use it. Let stand at room temperature for 5 minutes before serving.

This dressing will keep for up to 2 weeks in an airtight container in the refrigerator.

Makes about 1 1/4 cups

Louis Dressing

This dressing is based on an old American classic: crab Louis, which was made with crabmeat and a mayonnaise-based dressing. The dish is claimed by at least two different San Francisco hotel dining rooms, as well as by the chef at the Olympic Club in Seattle, Washington. The recipe harks back to the days when no one worried about calories, and the result was some very delicious eating.

> 1 cup mayonnaise (reduced-fat is acceptable)
> $1/4$ cup chili sauce
> 2 green onions, white part only, thinly sliced
> 1 teaspoon freshly squeezed lemon juice
> Salt and freshly ground pepper
> $1/4$ cup whipping cream

In a medium-size bowl, combine the mayonnaise, chili sauce, green onions, lemon juice, and salt and pepper to taste. Whisk together well. In a separate jar or bowl, whip the cream with a hand blender or mixer until soft peaks form. Whisk the cream into the mayonnaise mixture gently but thoroughly. Cover and chill the dressing until you are ready to use it. Let stand at room temperature for 5 minutes before serving. This dressing is at its best on the day it is made.

Makes about $1^1/2$ cups

Roasted Garlic Salad Dressing

Roasting garlic mellows its flavor, so don't be alarmed by the quantity used here.

I whole garlic bulb
I teaspoon extra virgin olive oil
3 tablespoons sour cream
2 tablespoons mayonnaise (reduced-fat is acceptable)
2 tablespoons plain yogurt
2 green onions, green part only, chopped
$1^1/_2$ tablespoons cider vinegar
Salt and freshly ground pepper

Preheat the oven to 375 F. Cut off the pointed top of the garlic bulb, removing about $^1/_2$ inch. Place cut side down on a piece of aluminum foil and drizzle with the oil. Wrap up in the foil and bake for 40 minutes. Let cool. Squeeze the garlic from the cloves.

In a jar with a hand blender or in a food processor fitted with a steel blade, combine the garlic puree with the remaining ingredients, adding salt and pepper to taste. Process until smooth. Cover and chill the dressing until you are ready to use it. Let stand at room temperature for 5 minutes before serving.

This dressing will keep for up to 4 days in an airtight container in the refrigerator.

Makes about $^3/_4$ cup

Green Goddess Dressing

Another American classic, this salad dressing is made with mayonnaise, anchovies, and tarragon. The dressing was created in the 1920s at the Palace Hotel in San Francisco at the request of an actor who was appearing in town in a play entitled "The Green Goddess." The play was later made into a film, but the dressing is more famous.

1½ cups mayonnaise (reduced-fat is acceptable)
½ cup loosely packed fresh parsley (preferably flat-leaf)
1 small onion, chopped
2 tablespoons cider vinegar
2 tablespoons chopped fresh tarragon, or 1 teaspoon dried
1½ tablespoons anchovy paste
3 tablespoons thinly sliced fresh chives

In a jar with a hand blender or in a food processor fitted with a steel blade, combine the mayonnaise, parsley, onion, vinegar, tarragon, and anchovy paste. Process until smooth. Stir in the chives. Cover and chill the dressing until you are ready to use it. Let stand at room temperature for 5 minutes before serving.

This dressing will keep for up to 5 days in an airtight container in the refrigerator.

Makes about 2½ cups

Creamy Pepper-Parmesan Salad Dressing

This creamy cheese dressing is flavored with lots of pepper. I usually make it with freshly grated Parmesan, but Romano makes a good substitute and is a nice change of pace.

$^1/_4$ cup mayonnaise (reduced-fat is acceptable)
$^1/_4$ cup milk
2 tablespoons freshly grated Parmesan cheese
2 tablespoons freshly squeezed lemon juice
1 tablespoon cider vinegar
1 tablespoon water
2 teaspoons minced onion
1 teaspoon freshly ground pepper
Dash of Tabasco sauce
Dash of Worcestershire sauce
Salt

Combine all the ingredients in a bowl or jar, adding salt to taste. Stir or shake well to combine. Cover and chill the dressing until you are ready to use it. Let stand at room temperature for 5 minutes before mixing again and serving.

This dressing will keep for up to 4 days in an airtight container in the refrigerator.

Makes about 1 cup

Creamy Dijon Salad Dressing

This dressing makes a great sauce for artichokes.

$1/2$ cup mayonnaise (reduced-fat is acceptable)
2 tablespoons red wine vinegar
1 clove garlic, finely chopped
2 teaspoons Dijon mustard
2 teaspoons Worcestershire sauce
1 teaspoon anchovy paste
Freshly ground pepper

Combine all the ingredients in a bowl or jar, adding pepper to taste. Stir or shake well to combine. Cover and chill the dressing until you are ready to use it. Let stand at room temperature for 5 minutes before serving.

This dressing will keep for up to 2 weeks in an airtight container in the refrigerator.

Makes about $3/4$ cup

Flatlander's Favorite

This dressing is very thick, with hard-boiled eggs giving the dressing its flavor and texture. It makes a very good dressing for asparagus. The combination of eggs and asparagus resonates with spring.

3 hard-cooked eggs, separated
3 tablespoons white wine vinegar
2 tablespoons Dijon mustard
6 tablespoons extra virgin olive oil
$^1/_3$ cup plain yogurt
3 green onions, white part only, minced
Salt and freshly ground pepper

In a medium-size bowl, combine 2 of the egg yolks with the vinegar and mustard and mash to a paste. Slowly add the oil while whisking constantly. Continue whisking until the dressing is emulsified. Chop the remaining egg whites and 1 egg yolk and stir into the dressing along with the yogurt, green onions, and salt and pepper to taste. Cover and chill the dressing until you are ready to use it. Let stand at room temperature for 5 minutes before serving.

This dressing will keep for up to 2 days in an airtight container in the refrigerator.

Makes 1$^1/_2$ cups

Creamiest Parmesan Dressing

Although blue cheese comes to mind when we think of cheese dressings, Parmesan lends great flavor to a dressing. This creamy Parmesan dressing makes a delicious dip for vegetables.

> $1/4$ cup mayonnaise (reduced-fat is acceptable)
> $1/4$ cup freshly grated Parmesan cheese
> 3 tablespoons white wine vinegar
> 2 tablespoons sour cream
> 2 tablespoons chopped fresh parsley (preferably flat-leaf)
> 1 tablespoon Dijon mustard
> Pinch of fines herbes
> Salt and freshly ground pepper
> $1/3$ cup any vegetable oil

In a small bowl, mix together the mayonnaise, Parmesan, vinegar, sour cream, parsley, mustard, herbs, and salt and pepper to taste. Whisk well. Slowly add the oil, whisking constantly, until the dressing is emulsified. Cover and chill the dressing until you are ready to use it. Let stand at room temperature for 5 minutes before serving.

This dressing will keep for up to 5 days in an airtight container in the refrigerator.

Makes about 1 1/2 cups

Bob's Blue Cheese Dressing

Blue cheese dressing is wonderful drizzled over thick slices of tomato and avocado.

$1/2$ cup mayonnaise (reduced-fat is acceptable)
5 tablespoons milk
Juice of $1/2$ lemon
1 tablespoon minced onion
1 clove garlic, minced
$1/2$ teaspoon Worcestershire sauce
$1/2$ cup crumbled blue cheese
Salt and freshly ground pepper

In a bowl or jar, combine the mayonnaise, milk, lemon juice, onion, garlic, and Worcestershire. Stir or shake to mix well. Add the cheese and stir lightly. Add salt and pepper to taste. Cover and chill the dressing until you are ready to use it. Let stand at room temperature for 5 minutes before serving.

This dressing will keep for up to 4 days in an airtight container in the refrigerator.

Makes about $1 1/4$ cups

Creamy Tofu Salad Dressing

I recommend silken tofu for this recipe; it's smooth and tender, delivering a truly superior consistency.

8 ounces tofu
2 tablespoons extra virgin olive oil
2 tablespoons freshly squeezed lemon juice
1 tablespoon soy sauce
2 cloves garlic, minced
1 teaspoon chopped fresh dill, or $1/4$ teaspoon dried
$1/2$ teaspoon chili powder
Freshly ground pepper

In a jar with a hand blender or in a food processor fitted with a steel blade, combine all the ingredients, adding pepper to taste. Process until smooth. Cover and chill the dressing until you are ready to use it. Let stand at room temperature for 5 minutes before serving.

This dressing will keep for up to 4 days in an airtight container in the refrigerator.

Makes about 1 $1/4$ cups

Sesame Tofu Salad Dressing

Unpeeled ginger can be stored in the refrigerator for up to 3 weeks. When preparing ginger, be careful to peel only the outer, tough skin.

4 ounces silken tofu, drained
$^1/_3$ cup plus 1 tablespoon plain yogurt
2 tablespoons freshly squeezed lemon juice
1 tablespoon tahini (see page 43)
1 tablespoon toasted sesame oil
3 green onions, white part only, sliced
2 teaspoons grated fresh ginger
2 teaspoons honey
Salt and freshly ground pepper

In a jar with a hand blender or in a food processor fitted with a steel blade, combine all the ingredients, adding salt and pepper to taste. Process until smooth. Cover and chill the dressing until you are ready to use it. Let stand at room temperature for 5 minutes before serving.

This dressing will keep for up to 4 days in an airtight container in the refrigerator.

Makes about 1$^1/_4$ cups

T's Saucy Tartar

This one's great for seafood salads and for dipping.

1 cup mayonnaise (reduced-fat is acceptable)
1 hard-boiled egg, chopped
$1/4$ cup sweet pickles, minced
2 tablespoons shallots, minced
2 tablespoons capers, drained and minced
2 tablespoons minced fresh parsley (preferably flat-leaf)
1 teaspoon Dijon mustard
1 teaspoon freshly squeezed lemon juice
1 teaspoon chopped fresh tarragon, or $1/2$ teaspoon dried
Dash of Worcestershire sauce
Salt and freshly ground pepper

In a bowl or jar, combine all the ingredients, adding salt and pepper to taste. Stir well. Cover and chill the dressing until you are ready to use it. Let stand at room temperature for 5 minutes before serving.

This dressing will keep for up to 1 week in an airtight container in the refrigerator.

Makes about $1^1/2$ cups